Gay and Lesbian Role Models

The Gallup's Guide to Modern Gay, Lesbian, & Transgender Lifestyle

Gay and Lesbian Role Models

by Jaime Seba

Mason Crest Publishers

MASON CREST PUBLISHERS INC.
370 Reed Road
Broomall, Pennsylvania 19008
(866)MCP-BOOK (toll free)
www.masoncrest.com

First Printing
9 8 7 6 5 4 3 2 1

Library of Congress Cataloging-in-Publication Data
Seba, Jaime.
  Gay and lesbian role models / by Jaime Seba. — 1st ed.
     p. cm. — (The Gallup's guide to modern gay, lesbian, & transgender life-style)
  Includes bibliographical references and index.
  ISBN 978-1-4222-1747-4   ISBN 978-1-4222-1758-0 (series)
  ISBN 978-1-4222-1867-9 (pbk.)   ISBN 978-1-4222-1863-1 (pbk. series)

  1. Role models—Juvenile literature. 2. Gays—Juvenile literature. 3. Lesbians—Juvenile literature. I. Title.
  BF774.S43 2011
  306.76'6—dc22
                          2010014933

Produced by Harding House Publishing Service, Inc.
www.hardinghousepages.com
Interior design by MK Bassett-Harvey.
Cover design by Torque Advertising + Design.
Printed in the USA by Bang Printing.

PICTURE CREDITS

Contents

Introduction

We are both individuals and community members. Our differences define individuality; our commonalities create a community. Some differences, like the ability to run swiftly or to speak confidently, can make an individual stand out in a way that is viewed as beneficial by a community, while the group may frown upon others. Some of those differences may be difficult to hide (like skin color or physical disability), while others can be hidden (like religious views or sexual orientation). Moreover, what some communities or cultures deem as desirable differences, like thinness, is a negative quality in other contemporary communities. This is certainly the case with sexual orientation and gender identity, as explained in *Homosexuality Around the World*, one of the volumes in this book series.

Often, there is a tension between the individual (individual rights) and the community (common good). This is easily visible in everyday matters like the right to own land versus the common good of building roads. These cases sometimes result in community controversy and often are adjudicated by the courts.

An even more basic right than property ownership, however, is one's gender and sexuality. Does the right of gender expression trump the concerns and fears of a community or a family or a school? *Feeling Wrong in Your Own Body*, as the author of that volume suggests, means confronting, in the most personal way, the tension between individuality and community. And, while a community, family, and school have the right (and obligation) to protect its children, does the notion of property rights extend to controlling young adults' choice as to how they express themselves in terms of gender or sexuality?

Changes in how a community (or a majority of the community) thinks about an individual right or responsibility often precedes changes in the law enacted by legislatures or decided by courts. And for these changes to occur, individuals (sometimes working in small groups) often defied popular opinion, political pressure, or religious beliefs. Some of these trends are discussed in *A New Generation of Homosexuality*. Every generation (including yours!) stands on the accomplishments of our ancestors and in *Gay and Lesbian Role Models* you'll be reading about some of them.

One of the most pernicious aspects of discrimination on the basis of sexual orientation is that "homosexuality" is a stigma that can be hidden (see the volume about *Homophobia*). While some of my generation (I was your age in the early 1960s) think that life is so much easier being "queer" in the age of the Internet, Gay-Straight Alliances, and Ellen, in reality, being different in areas where difference matters is *always* difficult. Coming Out, as described in the volume of the same title, is always challenging—for both those who choose to come out and for the friends and family they trust with what was once a hidden truth. Being healthy means being honest—at least to yourself. Having supportive friends and family is most important, as explained in *Being Gay, Staying Healthy*.

Sometimes we create our own "families"—persons bound together by love and identity but not by name or bloodline. This is quite common in gay communities today as it was several generations ago. Forming families or small communities based on rejection by the larger community can also be a double-edged sword. While these can be positive, they may also turn into prisons of conformity. Does being lesbian, for example, mean everyone has short hair, hates men, and drives (or rides on) a motorcycle? *What Does It Mean to Be Gay, Lesbian, Bisexual, or Transgender?* "smashes" these and other stereotypes.

Another common misconception is that "all gay people are alike"—a classic example of a stereotypical statement. We may be drawn together because of a common prejudice or oppression, but we should not forfeit our individuality for the sake of the safety of a common identity, which is one of the challenges shown in *Gay People of Color: Facing Prejudices, Forging Identities*.

Coming out to who *you* are is just as important as having a group or "family" within which to safely come out. Becoming knowledgeable about these issues (through the books in this series and the other resources to which they will lead), feeling good about yourself, behaving safely, actively listening to others *and* to your inner spirit—all this will allow you to fulfill your promise and potential.

James T. Sears, PhD
Consultant

chapter 1

The Importance of Role Models

When Eric Alvarez was a growing up in Southern Florida, he was a popular athlete at his Catholic high school. He had lots of friends, made good grades, and had a bright future. He admired sports figures such as Dan Marino, Wayne Gretzky, and Magic Johnson. But no matter how much he tried to be like them, he always knew they weren't quite like him.

"I did not have any gay role models growing up, and I believe that kept me in the closet much longer than I would have liked," said Alvarez, who didn't begin coming out until he was twenty-five years old. "I would have enjoyed my life much more in my teens and early twenties if I had been free of the lies and deceit that existed in my life because I was so afraid to come out. And that was all because I was afraid that I was the only one."

After graduating college, Alvarez traveled all over the world and experienced many diverse cultures, which helped him accept and embrace his identity as a gay man. The more he saw and related to other gay people, the more comfortable he became with his own identify. Now a successful openly gay professional, he owns two homes with Jeff, his partner of more than ten years. They volunteer their time to support gay rights organizations, community development, and animal rescue initiatives. Looking back, Alvarez understands how different his life would have been if he'd had a gay role model to look up to when he was younger.

"Role models help youth develop by providing positive examples of achievable goals and careers," he said. "When children think they are alone or that

All children need role models in their lives— people they can look up to, people they can imitate, people they look to for guidance and advice.

no one is like them, it creates doubt and a lack of confidence which ultimately can stunt their development. I know that was the case for me. A positive role model would have assured me that it was okay to come out of the closet and be myself."

All young people need strong, positive influences in their lives, to help guide and direct them. This is especially necessary for those who don't identify with traditional heterosexual figures or images. When they begin to accept their homosexuality, many gay people look for others who share the same lifestyle, values, and personal characteristics. Some are fortunate enough to have role models in their community—teachers, friends, neighbors, and parents. And those connections can have a significant impact on personal development.

"I was raised in a very strict religion, and they had severe views against homosexuality," Monica Beckwith recalls. "But when I was a kid, my babysitter came out. I didn't understand what that meant, so I asked my mom about it, and she told me that he was gay. Then she told me I might hear bad things about him, but I should ignore them and just remember that he's my friend and I love him, no matter what. I didn't really understand it back then. But fifteen years later, when I came out to my mom, I knew I didn't have to be afraid."

Unfortunately, though, many people don't have strong role models in their lives. Alvarez didn't know anyone who was gay, and he never heard positive messages that let him know being gay was okay. So he responded by working extra hard to be accepted by his straight peers. And sometimes that meant doing whatever it took to fit in and not seem out of place with his friends.

"I knew I was different, but I didn't know what to do about it," Alvarez recalls. "Unfortunately, in high school, I did make fun of kids who were **effeminate** so no one would think I was gay, because that's what the other guys were doing. Although I was never very harsh, I do regret that behavior. I just didn't know what else to do. I wasn't ready to let everyone know I was different."

As it turned out, he wasn't actually alone. Years later, he learned that some of his former classmates had also faced the same challenge. And it made him realize how different their lives would have been if they'd been able to accept themselves, their similarities, and their differences.

"I wish I would have taken the lead and come out of the

What's That Mean?

Effeminate means that a man has the qualities that are culturally considered to be more suited to a woman than to a man. People often think that a man who is effeminate is automatically gay, but that is not the case. Some men who have more feminine qualities are gay, some are straight—and some very masculine men are straight, and some are gay.

closet," he said. "Having a role model would have let me know that it was okay. It would have made a big difference. So I know why it's so important to be a positive role model for other people."

Many young people face **intolerance** and ignorance in the halls of their schools, from their classmates and their teachers, administrators, and even guidance counselors. Some major religions continue to teach that homosexuality is a sin, making it impossible for young people to gain support or understanding. And parents often struggle to understand the issues and complexities of raising a gay child. But as more people join in the national discussion on gay issues, they spread awareness and understanding.

What's That Mean?

Intolerance is the refusal to accept differences in others, which includes an unwillingness to grant equal political, social, professional, and religious rights to those who are different.

Something that is *strident* commands attention by being loud, annoying, and harsh.

Rhetoric is verbal conversation.

"One of the benefits of today's public dialogue about homosexuality is that we can learn to be more comfortable with the subject," wrote Betty DeGeneres, mother of out actress Ellen DeGeneres, in her book *Just a Mom*. "While much of the talk is **strident,** hateful **rhetoric**, more and more we're hearing calm

What's That Mean?

Something that is *pivotal* is vitally important. A "pivot" is literally a shaft or pin on which something turns, so the word "pivotal" has to do with having a central function with the power to turn or change society.

Inclusion means that someone or something has been taken in as a full member of a larger group.

voices of reason. Since it is an unalterable, scientific fact that 3–10 percent of the world's population is homosexual, all parents should be aware that one or more of their children could grow up to be gay."

As gay rights issues and culture continue to receive increased attention nationwide, gay leaders have more and more opportunities to play *pivotal* roles in the development of gay youth. Since the 1970s, numerous individuals in politics, entertainment, and religion have stepped forward to speak out for gay rights and *inclusion*.

"(Role models) are very important," Episcopalian Bishop Gene Robinson said. "(Openly-gay politician) Harvey Milk was the first person in my consciousness, in his example as a gay rights leader and role model. It's important to appreciate those who came before and to acknowledge how much we stand on the shoulders of those who paved roads before us."

Robinson himself became a role model to many in the gay and lesbian community when he became one of the first openly gay *bishops*. People around the world recognized this as a unifying event, as they finally saw a way to **reconcile** their religious beliefs with their sexual orientation.

For many people, though, Hollywood holds the most influential figures in popular culture. Everything from catch phrases to hairstyles is dictated by the glitterati strolling down the red carpet and the characters seen by millions on television. While some celebrities revel in the **frivolity** of being rich and famous, others take that responsibility seriously, actively participating in health and human rights issues. Likewise, many straight celebrities have spoken publicly about the need for equal rights for their gay friends and colleagues.

"I have so many friends who are homosexual and I just adore these people. Period," said singer Alanis Morissette, who changed the lyrics of her hit song "Ironic" to be more inclusive of gays. "Anytime I can support the gay community in whichever way I can, I want to really show up big."

Some gay and lesbian actors hesitate to come out

What's That Mean?

Bishops are Anglican (Episcopal), Eastern Orthodox, or Roman Catholic religious leaders who rank above a priest and have authority to govern a geographical region within the church.

To **reconcile** means to restore friendship and harmony between two opposing outlooks or people.

Frivolity refers to things that are silly, lighthearted, or shallow.

Nathan Lane has become a positive role model for young gays.

because they fear the repercussions doing so may have on their careers, but many have recognized the need for positive gay role models in the mainstream. Although actor Nathan Lane came out privately to friends and family years before, and he'd portrayed gay characters in his career, he was prompted to acknowledge his sexual orientation publicly after the 1998 hate crime murder of Matthew Shepard, a gay twenty-one-year-old student at the University of Wyoming. The event touched Lane so deeply that he saw in it an opportunity to finally take a stand and be a positive influence at a very dark time.

"It was like somebody slapped me awake," Lane told the gay magazine *The Advocate.* "At this point, it's selfish not to do whatever you can. . . . If I do this story and say I'm a gay person, it might make it easier for someone else."

FIND OUT MORE ON THE INTERNET

Dispelling Myths of Homosexuality
www.mcgill.ca/studenthealth/information/
queerhealth/myths/

Homosexual Role Models
able2know.org/topic/121009-1

Not So Different
not-so-different.blogspot.com/2007/01/on-gay-role-models-other-day-i-posted.html

READ MORE ABOUT IT

Jennings, Kevin. *Becoming Visible: A Reader in Gay and Lesbian History for High School and College Students.* New York: Alyson, 2004.

Jennings, Kevin. *One Teacher in Ten: Gay and Lesbian Educators Tell Their Stories.* New York: Alyson, 2004.

chapter 2

Role Models in Hollywood

J ulie remembers being glued to her television set one night in 1997, watching the popular sit-com, *Ellen*. For a few months, Julie had been struggling with understanding her own sexuality and where she fit in the world. She didn't know many people who were gay, but she felt a connection to the actress portraying the title character on her favorite show, comedian Ellen DeGeneres.

That night, the episode was set in an airport, and the main character Ellen Morgan declared "I'm gay" to a crowd of people as she accidentally spoke into a microphone. The amusing scene was even more shocking than it was funny, because it marked the first time a main character came out on a major network television show. The episode made head-lines around the world, and it also marked a massive change in Julie's life.

"Ellen DeGeneres was a huge role model for me," Julie said. "Her coming out episode on her sitcom was amazing and gave me courage to do the same. She gave me a feeling of pride, in myself and in what it means to be gay. I'll never forget it."

Of course, not everyone was so pleased. **Homophobic** groups, including many religious organizations, protested the episode and boycotted sponsors of the show. Still, other Hollywood notables who appeared in the episode demonstrated plenty of support for the controversial move, including Laura Dern, Oprah Winfrey, Billy Bob Thornton, Demi Moore, k.d. lang, Gina Gershon, Jorja Fox, Leisha Hailey, Kathy Najimy, Jenny Shimizu, and Melissa Etheridge, along with Ellen's mother, Betty. Laura Dern, who is straight, played Ellen's love interest. Though she suffered from a lack of work in Hollywood following the landmark episode that she attributed to the negative backlash, Dern still considered it "an extraordinary experience and opportunity."

Since that episode first aired in 1997, the same year DeGeneres herself came out on *The Oprah Winfrey Show* and in *Time* magazine, she has frequently found herself at the forefront of the gay rights movement. After becoming a hugely popular daytime talk

What's That Mean?

Homophobic has to do with the fear and hatred of homosexuality.

Ellen DeGeneres is admired by many young people, straight and gay alike.

show host and then a judge on *American Idol*, DeGeneres quickly became one of the most recognizable gay role models in America.

Her Emmy-winning television talk show averaged

more than 3.3 million viewers in 2007, including many suburban housewives and other people who may not have had any other exposure to gay people, issues, or news items. Ellen often includes her mother, Betty, in discussions on the show, making her relatable to an even wider audience. In many ways, she is a role model for them, as well.

Bullying is taken seriously in schools today—but it continues to exist, and gay students are often the targets.

"I am reminded of the woman who wrote to Ellen after the coming-out episode," Betty recalled. "She learned her son was gay when he was seventeen years old. 'We're so glad he still has two years at home,' she said, 'so we can make him know what a great person he is.' This mother did the best and most loving thing she could do when she learned her child was gay. Determined to make her son feel good about himself, she built his self-esteem, bolstered his feelings of self-worth, and let him know he would always be loved for who he is. And in doing so, she lived the meaning of love."

Delivering that type of message is very important to Ellen DeGeneres. In February 2008, when openly gay eighth-grader Lawrence King was shot and killed in Oxnard, California, DeGeneres immediately discussed the incident on the air. After explaining that King's fourteen-year-old classmate Brandon McInerney's alleged motive was homophobia, a teary DeGeneres used the opportunity to make a broader statement about the state of intolerance and hate-based crimes in America.

"When the message out there is so horrible, that to be gay, you can get killed for it, then we have to change the message," she said. "Larry was not a second-class citizen. I am not a second-class citizen. It is okay that you're gay. I don't care what people say. I don't care what people think. . . .

What's That Mean?

A *monologue* is when only one person talks; in this context, it refers to a stand-up comedian's act.

"I would like you to start paying attention to how often being gay is the punch line of a *monologue*, or how often gay jokes are in a movie. That kind of message, laughing at someone because they're gay, is just the beginning. It starts with laughing at someone, then it's verbal abuse, then it's physical abuse, and then it's this kid Brandon killing a kid like Larry. We

Ellen DeGeneres and her partner, Portia de Rossi.

must change our country. And we can do it. We can do it with our behavior. We can do it with our messages that we send our children."

Being such a visible figure on the forefront of the gay rights movement can be an intimidating responsibility for some. That was the case for Australian actress Portia de Rossi. Known for her dry comedic delivery, de Rossi starred in television's *Ally McBeal*, *Arrested Development,* and *Better Off Ted,* routinely playing sultry, alluring, powerful, and straight women. She had been interested in DeGeneres for some time, but she was concerned about openly dating the high profile icon.

"I had met Ellen . . . and there was definitely a lot of chemistry between us, but I didn't allow myself to think of being with her just because of the place I was at," she told *The Advocate*. "I was still on *Ally McBeal* and still closeted and this seemed inconceivable. But I really never stopped thinking about her, because I just haven't felt that kind of energy with anyone in my life."

A year into her relationship with DeGeneres, de Rossi made the decision to come out publicly in 2005. It didn't take much time for her to recognize the impact out celebrities have as leaders in the gay community, and she realized just how important DeGeneres is to the many people who look to her as a gay role model.

EXTRA INFO

Proposition 8 (or the California Marriage Protection Act) was a ballot proposition and constitutional amendment passed in California in the November 2008, state elections. The measure added a new provision to the California Constitution. The new section reads: "Only marriage between a man and a woman is valid or recognized in California."

By restricting the definition of marriage to opposite-sex couples, the proposition overturned the California Supreme Court's earlier ruling that same-sex couples have a constitutional right to marry. California's state constitution put Proposition 8 into immediate effect the day after the election. The proposition did not affect domestic partnerships in California.

People in favor of Proposition 8 argued that exclusively heterosexual marriage was "an essential institution of society," and that allowing same-sex marriages to have legal status would "result in public schools teaching our kids that gay marriage is okay," and that "gays . . . do not have the right to redefine marriage for everyone else." Opponents argued that "the freedom to marry is fundamental to our society," that the California constitution "should guarantee the same freedom and rights to everyone," and that the proposition "mandates one set of rules for gay and lesbian couples and another set for everyone else." They also argued that "equality under the law is a fundamental constitutional guarantee."

The campaigns for and against Proposition 8 raised $39.9 million and $43.3 million, respectively, the highest-funded campaign on any state ballot that day and surpassing every campaign in the country in spending except the presidential contest. After the elections, demonstrations and protests occurred across the state and nation. Same-sex couples filed numerous lawsuits with the California Supreme Court, challenging the proposition's validity and effect on previously administered same-sex marriages. As a result, the court upheld Proposition 8, but allowed same-sex couples who had gotten married before Proposition 8 was passed to still be considered legally married.

"It's hard having a relationship that's public. It's hard living a life that's somewhat public, and hard when you put that life together with someone who is so famous and so loved and admired. It's also real exciting," she said. "Just being a couple—being able to walk down a red carpet holding her hand, that's exciting for me."

Beyond exciting, she also saw another level to the impact that fame and recognition had on the lives of ordinary people.

"I respect her so much," de Rossi said of DeGeneres. "She was so courageous and so loud in '97, and now she is doing something that is more *subliminal.* She's changing the world, she really is, and it's exciting to be a part of that. . . . If I was

What's That Mean?

Subliminal has to do with perceptions or reactions that take place just below our conscious awareness.

fourteen and knew some gay people, I wouldn't nearly have had the struggle I had. Our world is definitely changing."

As the debate over same-sex marriage rights ignited in the United States, DeGeneres and deRossi were increasingly looked to as a model couple. And millions of fans celebrated with them when a May 2008 ruling by the California Supreme Court legalized same-sex marriage in that state.

"If you haven't heard, the California Supreme Court overturned a ban on gay marriage. So I would like to say right now, for the first time, I am announcing I am getting married," DeGeneres declared on her talk show to a wildly cheering audience that included de Rossi. "It's something that we've wanted to do, and we want it to be legal, and we're just very, very excited."

Shortly after, the couple shared their wedding video on national television and did a joint interview with Oprah Winfrey. Though the California Supreme Court decision was reversed in 2008 when voters passed Proposition 8 outlawing same-sex marriage, their marriage remains valid.

For Eric Alvarez, whose decade-long relationship is not legally recognized, being able to share even just a small part of the celebrity couple's marriage was a joy. And, more important, it spoke volumes about the advancement of gay rights since his youth.

"Her success has shown that it is okay to be different," Alvarez said of DeGeneres. "There are definitely more role models today than in the past, which has led to more gays and lesbians coming out of the closet at an earlier age. Advances in equal rights for gays and lesbians are due to the further acceptance of gays and lesbians in society. And that is because of the visibility of gay role models and the destruction of old **stereotypes**. Ellen played a huge role in moving that forward."

Other celebrities joined DeGeneres and de Rossi during the less than six months when same-sex marriages were legally conducted in California. One was George Takei, Mr. Sulu on the original *Star Trek* television series, who learned of the Supreme Court decision while at home with Brad, his partner of twenty-one years.

"We were in the kitchen and we had the TV going, and when the word came down suddenly Brad got on

What's That Mean?

Stereotypes are simplified, often negative mental images applied to all members of a group. Since all people are individuals, stereotypes are almost always inaccurate—and they also tend to be expressions of prejudice against particular groups. Examples of stereotypes would be: "All blondes are dumb." "Jocks are bad at schoolwork." "Blacks aren't as educated as whites." "Gay guys are effeminate." "Lesbians are masculine." None of these stereotypes are true for every member (or even most members) of the group to which they refer.

his knees in front of me," Takei told *People* magazine. "And I said, 'What are you doing?' He said, 'George, will you marry me?' I said 'Yes. You beat me to it. I meant to ask you.'"

Addressing a crowd of supporters after getting the marriage license in West Hollywood, Takei announced, "May equality live long and prosper."

Naomi Peters had struggled to find common ground with her parents after coming out to them. Then her mother, an avid *Star Trek* fan, read an article about Takei's marriage, accompanied by a photo of the happy couple with former cast-mates Leonard Nemoy, Walter "Chekov" Koenig, and Nichelle "Uhura" Nichols, who were among the guests.

"When my mom saw online that Mr. Sulu got married to another man, and his friends were there to support him, she called me to tell me about it," Peters said. "She said, 'How nice for him. He looks so happy!' I couldn't believe it. For some reason, that helped her put everything into perspective and understand me better."

Comedian Wanda Sykes was married to her partner in a private ceremony in October 2008, but she decided to step into the spotlight and come out publicly the following month as part of a demonstration against California's Proposition 8. As one of the few out African American celebrities in Hollywood, she felt a responsibility to be open about her life in

George Takei and his partner on their wedding day.

public. She wasn't looking forward to it in the beginning, but by the end, she had no regrets.

"I was out at work; I was out to my family; I was out to my friends. I lived my life as a lesbian," she said of her coming out. "But because I'm a celebrity I have to do this additional step, which is to tell total strangers that I'm a lesbian. . . . I didn't know it would be this liberating."

Similarly, Neil Patrick Harris lived openly gay in his personal life prior to publicly acknowledging his homosexuality to *People* magazine in 2006. "I am happy to dispel any rumors or misconceptions and am quite proud to say that I am a very content gay man living my life to the fullest and feel most fortunate to be working with wonderful people in the business I love," said Harris, who rose to stardom as a child actor playing the title role in the television show *Doogie Howser, M.D.*

Many actors have expressed concern that coming out would limit the roles they are able to play, fearing they might be branded as being able to play only gay characters. But Harris, who began playing the role of **lecherous**, womanizing single guy Barney on the popular television show *How I Met Your Mother* in 2005, demonstrated that this isn't the case. Fans seemed to easily separate Harris from his small screen alter ego, as the show climbed in the ratings and earned an average of more than eight million viewers for the 2006 season. Harris recognizes that this acceptance was due, at least in part, to other gay role models coming out publicly.

"Clearly there's way more exposure and a much larger gray area with sexuality and the public's opinion towards it—on almost every level—professionally, artistically, legally," he said in *Out* magazine. "What made it more unique 20 years ago was that there were less examples—so that made it a shock. And I think the shock value has kind of worn off."

And Harris has come to terms with being a role model, a job he never asked for and wasn't sure he wanted.

"I'm striving to be an example of normalcy," he said. "Because I'm noticed as an actor, people are aware of what's happening in my life, and that I can't change, and if I tried to, it'd be an uphill battle. . . . I'm a big proponent of **monogamous** relationships regardless of sexuality, and I'm proud of how the nation is steering toward that."

Considering the massive impact celebrities have on our culture and popular attitudes, the ever-growing number of proudly and publicly gay stars in Hollywood has had a ripple effect on mainstream

What's That Mean?

Someone who is *lecherous* expresses sexual lust in a way that is inappropriate and offensive.

Monogamous has to do with having only one sexual partner at a time.

Rufus Wainright is just one of the many celebrities who have publicly come out.

Americans. The volume sometimes matters even more than the individual.

"There are thousands of televisions shows, magazines, and websites dedicated to celebrities. They basically dictate what's acceptable in our culture," said Alvarez, who experiences this firsthand from his home in Los Angeles. "So when average people can list five or ten or more Hollywood stars who also happen to be gay, it helps people recognize that someone being gay isn't really that big of a deal. It's just one part of who they are."

Among those celebrities who have publicly discussed their homosexuality are musicians Lance Bass, *American Idol* runners-up Clay Aiken and Adam Lambert, *Sex and the City* star Cynthia Nixon, comedian Lily Tomlin, director John Waters, singer Rufus Wainright, television host Steve Kmetko, *Frasier* and Broadway star David Hyde Pierce, *M*A*S*H* actor David Ogden Stiers, comedian Rosie O'Donnell, actor T.R. Knight, Savage Garden frontman Darren Hayes, producer David Geffen, actor Rupert Everett, reality show host Tim Gunn, Judas Priest vocalist Rob Halford, and director Gus Van Sant.

"Every time someone recognizable comes out, it's like the whole community takes a step forward," Alvarez said. "When people start to realize that 'gay' means someone in their favorite band or on their favorite television show, then suddenly it's not such a big deal when it means their neighbor, too."

FIND OUT MORE ON THE INTERNET

Ellen Degeneris on People.com
www.people.com/people/ellen_degeneres

The Ellen Degeneris Show
ellen.warnerbros.com

READ MORE ABOUT IT

Degeneres, Ellen. *The Funny Thing Is . . .* New York: Simon & Schuster, 2004.

Degeneres, Ellen. *My Point . . . And I Do Have One.* New York: Bantam, 2007.

chapter 3

Role Models in Politics and Religion

When President-elect Barack Obama was inaugurated on January 18, 2009, it was an historic event as America ushered in the era of its first black president. As the day of ceremony began, it was kicked off with a prayer by New Hampshire Episcopal Bishop Gene Robinson.

"Bless this nation with anger at *discrimination* at home and abroad, against refugees and immigrants, women, people of color, gay, lesbian, bisexual, and transgender people," he prayed. "Bless us with discomfort at the easy *simplistic* answers we prefer to hear from our politicians instead of the truth

What's That Mean?

Discrimination is the unfair treatment of a person or group of people based on prejudice.

Something that is *simplistic* is not complex enough to explain the true meaning of something; it is *too* simple.

about ourselves and our world, which we need to face if we are going to rise to the challenges of the future."

Addressing a crowd in front of the Lincoln Memorial, Robinson stood as a living example that a devotion to religion doesn't have to be separate from being gay. He recognized the significance of the location, where Dr. Martin Luther King Jr. had delivered his historic "I have a dream" speech.

"It's important for any minority to see themselves represented in some way," Robinson told the *Concord (N.H.) Monitor*. "Whether it be a racial minority, an ethnic minority or, in our case, a sexual minority, just seeing someone like you up front matters."

Biship Gene Robinson has a groundbreaking role as the first openly gay leader of a Christian church.

Robinson became known around the globe in 2003 when he became the world's first openly gay Episcopal bishop. But his struggle to reconcile his gay self with his spiritual life began much earlier. He was married and raising two children when he came out in the 1980s. He and his wife remained friends but divorced. In 1987, he met his partner and they began living together. A year later, Robinson became Canon to the Ordinary, or Assistant to the Bishop, and remained in that post until he was elected Bishop of the Episcopal Diocese of New Hampshire on June 7, 2003.

"I think my election is one of several indications that gay and lesbian folk are being brought more into the center of things. I'd like to think that my election signals my bringing of gay and lesbian folk into the center of the church," he said. "It's not about me. It's about not having to be ashamed."

The event brought a storm of controversy and division within the Episcopalian/Anglican church in the United States and worldwide. Robinson received death threats and hate mail, and the storm has continued for years.

"If indeed this is the work of God . . . then it's a crisis that calls for the church to be its very best self, and not worry about risking itself for the right thing," Robinson said. "Sometimes there are things worth risking your life for. It was Jesus who said if you want to save your life, you have to lose it."

EXTRA INFO

"I Have a Dream" is the name given to the public speech by Martin Luther King Jr., in which he called for racial equality and an end to discrimination. King made the speech on August 28, 1963, from the steps of the Lincoln Memorial during the March on Washington for Jobs and Freedom; it is considered to be a defining moment in the American Civil Rights Movement. Delivered to over 200,000 civil rights supporters, the speech is also considered to be one of the greatest speeches in history. According to U.S. Representative John Lewis, who also spoke that day as the president of the Student Non-Violent Coordinating Committee, "Dr. King had the power, the ability, and the capacity to transform those steps on the Lincoln Memorial into a monumental area that will forever be recognized. By speaking the way he did, he educated, he inspired, he informed not just the people there, but people throughout America and unborn generations."

Here are some of the most powerful lines from the speech:

"I have a dream that one day this nation will rise up and live out the true meaning of its creed: 'We hold these truths to be self-evident, that all men are created equal.'"

"I have a dream that my four little children will one day live in a nation where they will not be judged by the color of their skin, but by the content of their character."

"I have a dream that one day on the red hills of Georgia the sons of former slaves and the sons of former slave owners will be able to sit down together at a table of brotherhood."

"Now is the time to lift our nation from the quicksand of racial injustice to the solid rock of brotherhood. Now is the time to make justice a reality for all of God's children."

In a country that claims a separation of church of state as a prized value, Robinson's presence at the inauguration was a meaningful fusing of the two. And it served as a reminder that politics and religion are often linked, especially when it comes to gay issues. Frequently, debates over public policies and legal rulings related to gay rights are rooted in **conservative** religious values.

For gay and lesbian people, this makes positive role models in both politics and religion extremely important. Having voices on both sides speaking out about tolerance and acceptance helps improve unity and understanding.

One of the most high-profile political leaders advocating for lesbian and gay rights is Congressman Barney Frank, who was first elected to the U.S. House of Representatives as a Massachusetts Democrat in 1981. He has

What's That Mean?

Someone who is *conservative* is in favor of keeping things the way they have always been, sticking close to tradition rather than being open to change and new ideas.

frequently been a leader on gay and lesbian rights, especially since coming out in 1987.

"I'm used to being in the minority," he said. "I'm a left-handed gay Jew. I've never felt, automatically, a member of any majority."

Frank has also challenged commonly held ideas about the influence religion should have on politics. In 1984, during an all-night House Floor debate on school prayer, Republican Representative Marjorie Holt from Maryland declared, "This is a Christian nation."

Frank, who was chairing the debate at the request of the House leadership, responded, "If this is a Christian nation, how come some poor Jew has to get up at 5:30 in the morning to preside over the House of Representatives?"

That type of wit has garnered Frank much attention when he responds to attacks and accusations by colleagues and the media. When a 2009 article in *The New Yorker* reported that he supported a "*radical*" homosexual *agenda*, Frank again gave a biting response.

What's That Mean?

Someone or something that is *radical* is in favor of bringing about extreme changes in the status quo.

An *agenda* is an underlying plan or program based on ideas and beliefs.

A *platform*, when used in this context, means a declaration of principles and policies upon which a group of people stands.

"I do not think that any self-respecting radical in history would have considered advocating people's rights to get married, join the Army, and earn a living as a terribly inspiring revolutionary *platform*," he said.

As of 2010, Frank was one of three openly gay members of Congress. In 1999, Tammy Baldwin was elected to the House of Representatives as a Democrat from Wisconsin's second congressional

Jared Polis, an openly gay man, was elected to the House of Representatives in 2008.

district, and Democrat Jared Polis became the first openly gay man elected to the House from Colorado's second district in 2008.

Baldwin recognizes the importance of role models, because as a young woman, she was inspired by a trailblazing leader.

"I was twenty-two years old, very interested in politics, but I didn't really know what my options were," she said. "That 1984 convention was the one where the Democrats nominated Geraldine Ferraro, the first woman, to run for vice president. I was so excited. So there I was, in my little apartment, watching Geraldine Ferraro delivering her acceptance speech and thinking, 'Wow, I can do anything in politics. The barriers are being broken. The sky's the limit."

She had the opportunity to meet her role model many years later. "I told her I probably wouldn't be in Congress if I hadn't seen her speech," Baldwin said. "I would be so happy if I could do for someone else what she did for me."

Although the fight for gay rights and the acceptance of gays in politics continues in the United States, elsewhere in the world gay leaders have risen to influential positions in government. At the young age of thirty-four, 1998, multi-millionaire British media *entrepreneur* Waheed Alli became the first openly gay *peer* in the British Parliament and one of the world's few openly gay Muslim leaders. And in 2009, Iceland welcomed the world's first openly gay head of government in the modern era, Jóhanna Sigurðardóttir. While this was a historic international event, Icelanders were too focused on the financial crisis facing their country to be concerned about the new prime minister's private life.

"Being gay is not an issue in Iceland," Frosti Jónsson, chairman of Iceland's gay-and-lesbian association, told *Time* magazine. "There are so many openly gay prominent figures in both the public and private *sector* here that it doesn't affect who we select for our highest offices. Our minds are focused on what counts, which is the current situation in the country."

Gay rights *activists* look forward to a time when Americans will follow Iceland's example, and adopt

What's That Mean?

Activists are people who are willing to take action to bring about change.

a similar sentiment in the United States. For that to occur, role models who accept the responsibility of being leaders in the gay community will play a pivotal role. Baldwin now has that opportunity, as a high profile and influential leader in politics.

"There's a powerful [part] for role models to play in terms of inspiring **LGBT** people who question whether their identity might in some way **impede** their reaching for the stars, reaching for their dreams," she said. "That's one element I'm proud of. . . . It's great to achieve historic firsts, but there's still work to be done until we achieve the seconds and the thirds and the fourths, until these achievements are commonplace and nobody thinks twice about them. We've come a long way. Now the hard work is to make this everyday news."

What's That Mean?

LGBT stands for lesbian, gay, bisexual, and transgender. It's an all-encompassing term used for the entire community of people who is not heterosexual.

Impede means to get in the way of.

FIND OUT MORE ON THE INTERNET

Congressman Barney Frank Official Website
www.house.gov/frank

Let God Love Gene Robinson
www.gq.com/news-politics/newsmakers/200806/gene-robinson-gay-bishop-protestant

READ MORE ABOUT IT

Adams, Elizabeth. *Going to Heaven: The Life and Election of Bishop Gene Robinson*. New York: Soft Skull Press, 2006.

Robinson, Gene V. *In the Eye of the Storm: Swept to the Center by God*. New York: Seabury Books, 2008.

Weisberg, Stuart. *The Barney Frank: The Story of America's Only Left-Handed Gay, Jewish Congressman*. Amherst, Mass.: University of Massachusetts Press, 2009.

chapter 4

Role Models in Sports

It's not difficult to understand why a professional athlete might decide to stay in the closet. It is an industry perceived to be dominated by straight men, and intolerance toward gays is common. Consider the opinions former NBA star Tim Hardaway made publicly on a radio show in 2007: "You know, I hate gay people, so I let it be known," Hardaway said. "I don't like gay people and I don't like to be around gay people. I am homophobic. I don't like it. It shouldn't be in the world or in the United States."

Although Hardaway later apologized for his comments, such attitudes are unfortunately not surprising in American professional sports—or, often, in America. So it makes sense that most professional athletes who do come out wait until their careers are over.

"If you look at our league, minorities aren't very well represented," Utah Jazz center John Amaechi said in 2002. "There's hardly any Hispanic players, no Asian Americans, so that there's no openly gay players is no real surprise. It would be like an alien dropping down from space. There'd be fear, then panic: they just wouldn't know how to handle it."

Some argue that is exactly why it is so important for gay athletes to stand up and be role models for others. Amaechi realized that. So, five years later, after he had retired from the league, Amaechi became the first NBA player to publicly come out.

John Amaechi's respectful stance on tolerance and diversity have made him an outstanding mentor for young adults.

Hardaway's comments came a week later. They were met by shock by some and agreement by others. But Amaechi himself stayed as fair-minded as he could.

"Finally, someone who is honest," Amaechi said of Hardaway's statement. "It is ridiculous, absurd, *petty*, *bigoted* and shows a lack of *empathy* that is *gargantuan* and *unfathomable*. But it is honest. And it illustrates the problem better than any of the fuzzy language other people have used so far."

In his book, *Man in the Middle,* Amaechi described that problem in the league: "It's a testosterone-riddled group. It's not just the NBA, it's professional sports."

That was what inspired him to come out. And the response was far from universally negative. Amaechi's courage in taking a stand prompted several of his former teammates and colleagues in the NBA to make public statements of support. He became a role model for them, too.

What's That Mean?

Petty means shallow, unimportant, and ungenerous.

Someone who is *bigoted* is blindly and obstinately attached to some creed or opinion, while being intolerant toward others.

Someone who demonstrates *empathy* is able to put himself in someone else's shoes, understanding and entering into others' feelings.

Gargantuan means huge, immense.

Something that is *unfathomable* is beyond being able to be understood or measured.

"The fact that John has done this, maybe it will give others the comfort or confidence to come out as well, whether they are playing or retiring," Amaechi's former teammate Grant Hill told the Associated Press.

Retired NBA superstar Charles Barkley agreed, and hoped players in his former profession would get with the times when it comes to the topic of gays in the league.

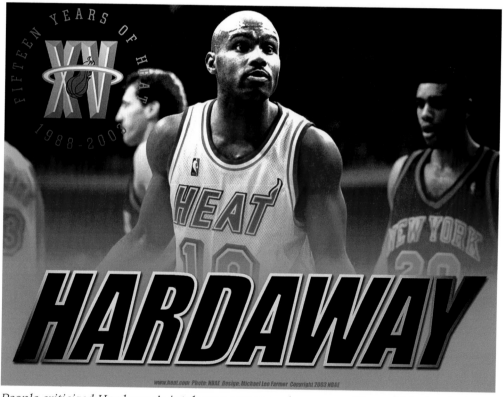

People criticized Hardaway's intolerant stance on homosexuality and felt that he had damaged the reputation of the NBA. Other players insisted that homosexuality has nothing to do one way or another with an athlete's ability to play.

Tennis player Martina Navratilova knows how important role models are to young people in the gay community.

"It shouldn't be a big deal to anybody," he said. "I know I've played with gay players and against gay players, and it just shouldn't surprise anybody or be any issue."

Amaechi's NBA coach Glenn "Doc" Rivers always considered him a role model, and the revelation about his homosexuality didn't change that.

"He's better than a good kid; he's a fantastic kid," Rivers said of Amaechi. "He did as much charity work as anybody in our city, and he's still doing it. That's what I wish we focused on. Unfortunately, we're talking about his sexual orientation, which I couldn't care a flying flip about."

Former tennis pro Martina Navratilova, who came out in 1981 at the height of her career, was glad to see Amaechi stand up and join the ranks of the few professional athletes who have come out and become leaders in the gay community.

"It's hugely important for the kids so they don't feel alone in the world," she said. "We're role models. He will definitely help a lot of kids growing up to feel better about themselves."

Openly gay women like Navratilova have traditionally been accepted more readily in professional sports than gay men, even in professional basketball. WNBA star and three-time Olympic gold medalist Sheryl Swoopes came out in 2005, when she was a forward with the Houston Comets. And she recognizes the unfair and biased attitudes faced by gay men in her profession.

"Male athletes of my **caliber** probably feel like they have a lot more to lose than gain [by coming out]," she said. "I don't agree with that. To me, the most important thing is happiness."

Billy Bean, a former professional baseball player with the Tigers, Dodgers, and Padres, came out in 1999, eight years after he retired. Like Amaechi, he recognized that the male-dominated world of professional sports wouldn't be open to an openly gay player.

What's That Mean?

Caliber means quality or degree of worth.

"Baseball, I knew, wasn't ready for a guy like me, no matter how well I played," Bean wrote in his book, *Going the Other Way.* "The game wasn't mature enough to deal with a gay ballplayer, and I wasn't in an emotional state to take it on by myself."

The feeling of being unable to stand up and be the first, or the only, person to come out in a sport is similar to the way thousands of gay people feel all over the world. Whether in the national spotlight or not, the process of coming out can be isolating and frightening. That was why Bean decided to write his book. He knew that he probably wasn't alone, and there would be others who would benefit from knowing his story.

"It's for anyone who has ever wanted to make their parents proud, play for the team, reach a goal, and be their best," he wrote about his book. "It's for parents who want to understand the struggles faced by their children. It's for athletes who are not sure they can deal with a gay teammate. It's for gay athletes who may feel, as I did, that no one else walked in their cleats or high-tops."

Navratilova similarly knew that her position as an internationally recognized athlete put her in a unique position to **advocate** for gay rights around the world. A native of Czechoslovakia, she won 168 singles titles, including eighteen Grand Slams. Since retiring, she has worked for gay rights issues and promoting women's health and fitness.

What's That Mean?

People who *advocate* for something stand up for something or push for it strongly.

"She's the greatest singles, doubles, and mixed doubles player who's ever lived," said openly gay former tennis player Billie Jean King. "When you think about her, you think about staying healthy. She's someone who is very comfortable in her own skin, about her sexuality, which I think is good for others to see."

Rudy Galindo also faced some challenges after coming out as a professional ice skater. And although it was easier in his sport than others, he believes gay

Professional ice skater Rudy Galindo believes it is important that gay athletes stand up openly for their identity, as role models to the next generation.

athletes are role models who benefit their community by being open about their lives.

"I just think a lot of those athletes can't come out because it's a team thing and they're just worried about **endorsements**," Galindo said. "I'm not going to say they're cowards. . . . I just think their sexual preference is no big deal."

For Galindo, he didn't just come out as gay. He risked his career and public image when he announced that he'd tested positive for HIV in 2000. Instead of letting the disease define him, Galindo continued to compete and demonstrate that the diagnosis was not the end of his world.

What's That Mean?

Endorsements are promotional statements. Athletes and other celebrities get paid lots of money for endorsing various products.

"You've got to be religious about it," he said. "I get up, do yoga, skate for a couple of hours, play racquetball with my sister, do weights, jumps on the floor, and then right before I go to bed, I do a half-hour cardio."

Galindo was inspired by another athletic role model, openly gay Olympic diver Greg Louganis. "After reading Greg Louganis's autobiography, I learned a lot about what an important position I was in as an openly gay competitive athlete, and how important it was for me not to appear as if I were in any way ashamed of or embarrassed by my sexual orientation," Galindo said.

Louganis made history in 1984 when he won two gold medals at the Summer Olympics in Los Angeles, and then repeated the achievement in the 1988 Olympics in Seoul, Korea. He was named "Athlete of the Year" by ABC's *Wide World of Sports* in 1988, the same year he tested positive for HIV. He credits his sport for helping him to take pride in himself, his abilities, and his sexual identity.

"When you're a kid growing up, and you think you're gay, you know that you're different; you're often teased and it can really destroy your self-esteem," he said. "But sports can be great for building self-esteem."

Whenever a professional athlete comes out publicly, it makes it easier for others to do the same. Former NFL defensive lineman Esera Tuaolo recognized his homosexuality publicly only after his career ended, and he saw the impact coming out has on the many people who look to professional sports figures as role models.

"What John did is amazing. He does not know how many lives he's saved by speaking the truth," Tuaolo said of Amaechi. "Living with all that stress and that depression, all you deal with as a closeted person, when you come out, you really truly free yourself."

FIND OUT MORE ON THE INTERNET

Gay Sports
gaylife.about.com/od/healthfitness/a/gaysports.htm

Gay Sports Fans and Athletes
www.outsports.com

READ MORE ABOUT IT

Amaechi, John. *Man in the Middle.* Holmes, Penn.: ESPN, 2007.

Simmons, Roy and Damon DiMarco. *Out of Bounds: Coming Out of Sexual Abuse, Addiction, and My Life of Lies in the NFL.* Cambridge, Mass.: Da Capo Press, 2006.

Tuaolo, Esera and John Rosengren. *Alone in the Trenches.* Naperville, Ill.: Sourcebooks, 2007.

BIBLIOGRAPHY

"2006-07 Primetime Wrap." *The Hollywood Reporter*, May 25, 2007.

Amaechi, John. *Man in the Middle.* Holmes, Penn.: ESPN, 2007.

Barrett, John. "Sean Hayes, What Took You So Long?" *The Huffington Post*, March 10, 2010.

Bean, Billy. *Going the Other Way: Lessons from a Life in and out of Major-League Baseball.* Cambridge, Mass.: Da Capo Press, 2003.

Bolcer, Julie. "Geffen Not Subject of 'You're So Vain.'" *The Advocate*, March 1, 2010.

Brandao, Rodrigo. "Gus Van Sant." *Gay Life (about.com)*.

Caplan, David. "Clay Aiken: I'm a Gay Dad." *People*, September 24, 2008.

Cathcart, Rebecca. "Boy's Killing, Labeled a Hate Crime, Stuns Town." *The New York Times,* February 23, 2008.

DeGeneres, Betty. *Just a Mom.* New York: Alyson Books, 2001.

Dillon, Nancy. "'May equality live long and prosper'—George Takei, New Yorkers Among Ca. gay rush." *Daily News,* June 18, 2008.

Franks, Alan. "Rufus Wainwright on love, loss and life in a musical dynasty." *The Times (UK)*, March 27, 2010.

Gorgan, Ellen. "Darren Hayes Marries Gay Partner." *Softpedia*, July 18, 2006.

Grossfeld, Stan. "Champions on Ice Skater Galindo rising above it all." *Boston Globe,* April 18, 2007.

Karpel, Ari. "Black and Gay Like Me." *The Advocate,* March 2009.

Keith, Bill. "A Man's Man." *Out,* August 2008.

Kirby, David. "Will the Real Out Celebrities Please Stand Up?" *The Advocate*, January 16, 2001.

Kort, Michele. "Portia Heart & Soul." *The Advocate.* September 13, 2005.

Louganis, Greg. *Breaking the Surface.* New York: Sourcebooks, Inc., 1995.

Mandel, Susan. "George Takei to Beam Up *Trek* Costars for Wedding." *People*, June 2, 2008.

Marikar, Sheila. "'M*A*S*H' Star David Ogden Stiers Reveals He's Gay." *ABC News*, May 6, 2009.

Moody, Jonas. "Iceland Picks World's First Openly Gay PM." *Time*, January 30, 2009.

Nichols, John. "Tammy Baldwin's Turn." *The Nation,* July 25, 2004.

Nylund, David. *Beers, Babes and Balls: Masculinity and Sports Talk Radio*. New York: State University of New York Press, 2007.

Parsley, Aaron. "Adam Lambert: I'm Gay." *People*, June 9, 2009.

Ross, Jonathan. "John Waters." *Guardian,* November 17, 1998.

Seidman, Robert. "Syndicated Top 25." *TV by the Numbers,* March 2010.

Shaw, Andrew. "The Royal Tour." *Melbourne Community Voice,* March 23, 2010.

Shulman, Randy. "Naked Gunn." *MetroWeekly*, September 27, 2007.

Singleton, Dave. "Q-and-A with Episcopalian Bishop Gene Robinson." *AARP.org,* June 2009.

Staff. "Coming out as a gay actor ruined my career in Hollywood, says actor Rupert Everett." *Daily Mail*, December 2, 2009.

Staff. "Cynthia Nixon right at home in gay relationship." *Daily News,* March 6, 2008.

Staff. "EXCLUSIVE: *Grey's Anatomy* star T.R. Knight Confirms He's Gay." People, October 19, 2006.

Staff. "Neil Patrick Harris 'I Am a Very Content Gay Man.'" *People,* November 20, 2006.

Staff. "Profile: Lord Waheed Alli." *BBC News,* November 29, 2000.

Staff. "Retired NBA star says he hates gay people." *ESPN*, February 16, 2007.

Thomson, Katherine. "David Hyde Pierce on His Marriage, Prop 8 Anger." *The Huffington Post,* 28 May 2009.

Timmins, Annamarie. "N.H. bishop invited to D.C. to give prayer." *Concord Monitor,* January 12, 2009.

Vilanch, Bruce. "Let Lily Tomlin Entertain You." *The Advocate*, January 2010.

Von Metzke, Ross. "Alanis Morissette Includes Gay Fans." *Gaydar-Radio.com*, June 2005.

Zoll, Rachel. "Only a call from God could keep gay bishop-elect from post, he says." *Associated Press*, October 23, 2003.

INDEX

ABOUT THE AUTHOR AND THE CONSULTANT

Jaime A. Seba's involvement in LGBT issues began in 2004, when she helped open the doors of the Pride Center of Western New York, which served a community of more than 100,000 people. As head of public education and outreach, she spearheaded one of the East Coast's first crystal methamphetamine awareness and harm reduction campaigns. She also wrote and developed successful grant programs through the Susan G. Komen Breast Cancer Foundation, securing funding for the region's first breast cancer prevention program designed specifically for gay, bisexual, and transgender women. Jaime studied political science at Syracuse University before switching her focus to communications with a journalism internship at the *Press & Sun-Bulletin* in Binghamton, New York, in 1999. She is currently a freelance writer based in Seattle.

James T. Sears specializes in research in lesbian, gay, bisexual, and transgender issues in education, curriculum studies, and queer history. His scholarship has appeared in a variety of peer-reviewed journals and he is the author or editor of twenty books and is the Editor of the *Journal of LGBT Youth*. Dr. Sears has taught curriculum, research, and LGBT-themed courses in the departments of education, sociology, women's studies, and the honors college at several universities, including: Trinity University, Indiana University, Harvard University, Penn State University, the College of Charleston, and the University of South Carolina. He has also been a Research Fellow at Center for Feminist Studies at the University of Southern California, a Fulbright Senior Research Southeast Asia Scholar on sexuality and culture, a Research Fellow at the University of Queensland, a consultant for the J. Paul Getty Center for Education and the Arts, and a Visiting Research Lecturer in Brazil. He lectures throughout the world.